Crisma y Cristián

Cathy Camarena, M.Ed., and Gloria B. Ruff, M.Ed.

Consulting Editors

Lourdes Flores-Hanson, M.S.E., and Gloria Rosso-White

ABDO
Publishing Company

Published by ABDO Publishing Company, 4940 Viking Drive, Edina, Minnesota 55435.

Printed in the United States.

Credits
Curriculum Coordinator: Nancy Tuminelly
Cover and Interior Design and Production: Mighty Media
Child Photography: Steven Wewerka, Wewerka Photography
Photo Credits: AbleStock, Brand X Pictures, Comstock, Anders Hanson, Tracy Kompelien, Photodisc, Stockbyte

Library of Congress Cataloging-in-Publication Data

Camarena, Cathy, 1966-
    Crisma y Cristián / Cathy Camarena, Gloria B. Ruff.
        p. cm. -- (Primeros sonidos)
    ISBN 1-59679-849-1 (hardcover)
    ISBN 1-59679-850-5 (paperback)
    1. Spanish language--Consonants--Juvenile literature. I. Ruff, Gloria B., 1971-
II. Title. III. Series.
    PC4159.C3455 2006
    468.1'3--dc22

                                                          2005053652

SandCastle™ books are created by a professional team of educators, reading specialists, and content developers around five essential components that include phonemic awareness, phonics, vocabulary, text comprehension, and fluency. All books are written, reviewed, and leveled for guided and early intervention reading, and designed for use in shared, guided, and independent reading and writing activities to support a balanced approach to literacy instruction.

Let Us Know

After reading the book, SandCastle would like you to tell us your stories about reading. What is your favorite page? Was there something hard that you needed help with? Share the ups and downs of learning to read. We want to hear from you! To get posted on the ABDO Publishing Company Web site, send us e-mail at:

sandcastle@abdopub.com

SandCastle Level: Beginning

ABCChDEFGH
IJKLLLMNÑOP
QRSTUVWXYZ

abcchdefgh
ijklllmnñop
qrstuvwxyz

Crisma

Cristián

creyones

crisálida

cremallera

cristal

crema

Veo los .

Esta es una .

Esta es una Y.

Mira el .

La es blanca.

Crisma usa los creyones.

A Crisma le gusta dibujar.

Cristián tiene un cristal.

El cristal es blanco.

Crisma dibuja el cristal de Cristián.

A Cristián le gusta el dibujó.

¿Cuáles de estas cosas comienzan con cr?

Más palabras que comienzan con cr

cráter

crisantemo

cronómetro

crucigrama

cruz

23

About SandCastle™

A professional team of educators, reading specialists, and content developers created the SandCastle™ series to support young readers as they develop reading skills and strategies and increase their general knowledge. The SandCastle™ series has four levels that correspond to early literacy development in young children. The levels are provided to help teachers and parents select the appropriate books for young readers.

Emerging Readers
(no flags)

Beginning Readers
(1 flag)

Transitional Readers
(2 flags)

Fluent Readers
(3 flags)

These levels are meant only as a guide. All levels are subject to change.

To see a complete list of SandCastle™ books and other nonfiction titles from ABDO Publishing Company, visit **www.abdopub.com** or contact us at:

4940 Viking Drive, Edina, Minnesota 55435 • 1-800-800-1312 • fax: 1-952-831-1632